NORFOLK COAST
FROM THE AIR

NORFOLK COAST
FROM THE AIR

Mike Page & Pauline Young

HALSGROVE

First published in Great Britain in 2006

British Library Cataloguing-in-Publication Data
A CIP record for this title is available from the British Library

ISBN 1 84114 430 4
ISBN 978 1 84114 430 6

HALSGROVE
Halsgrove House
Lower Moor Way
Tiverton, Devon EX16 6SS
Tel: 01884 243242
Fax: 01884 243325
email: sales@halsgrove.com
website: www.halsgrove.com

Printed and bound by D'Auria Industrie Grafiche Spa, Italy

FOREWORD

Mike Page's interests both in flying and photography make him particularly well qualified for aerial pictures. He has made three very successful videos of the Norfolk and Suffolk coastline from the air followed by a book of aerial pictures of The Broads, all with commentary and captions written by Pauline Young.

Now he has returned to the Norfolk coast. His brilliant and meticulously compiled images show its endlessly fascinating nature. Coastal villages, major and minor ports, cliffs, woodland, saltmarsh, nature reserves, seaside resorts – all are included.

The North Sea continues to shape the coastline which has been in a constant state of change ever since it became detached from mainland Europe millions of years ago.

You'll really enjoy these superb bird's-eye views of the coastline and Pauline Young's accompanying text.

James Hoseason OBE
Spring 2006

ACKNOWLEDGEMENTS

Our thanks go to the many organisations and individuals who have provided the information for this book. They include Roy Snelling (without whom the project would not have taken off in the first place), Keith Nunn, James Hoseason OBE, Patrick Lee, Jackie Routledge, Bob Malster, Judy Speed, the RSPB, King's Lynn Library, Norfolk County Archaeology Service, Air Traffic Control at Norwich Airport and fellow co-pilots from Seething Airfield.

And especially to our spouses Gillian Page and John Young for their tolerance and good humour throughout the preparation of this book.

Mike Page, Strumpshaw
Pauline Young, Norwich
Spring 2006

INTRODUCTION

I consider myself very fortunate. I'm Norfolk born and my two main interests outside my family are photography and flying. For over forty years I've been able to combine the two. In this collection of images of the Norfolk coast I've been privileged to be able to capture a wonderful variety of landscapes. Along the Norfolk coastline I've recorded seasonal changes such as saltmarshes in summer and winter, atmospheric conditions such as twilight at the Titchwell RSPB Reserve, and dramatic coastal erosion as at Happisburgh.

Digital photography has enabled me to store my thousands of images on computer; they're available to everyone as an archive. My camera is a Canon 1D Mk2 8.5 megapixel digital with a 2GB memory card. Canon 24-70 f2.8L and Canon 80-200 f2.8L lenses, both with UV filters, have proved an ideal combination for aerial photography. My camera is hand held so I need to use fast shutter speeds to counteract any turbulence. The ideal aircraft is a high-wing Cessna 150 which I fly with the window open. A safety pilot accompanies me to keep a lookout and fly the aircraft whilst I'm taking the pictures. I suppose I'm a perfectionist; if conditions aren't quite right I return to the scene and photograph it again and again until I'm satisfied with the quality of the picture.

I have worked with Pauline Young on many occasions. I supply the aerial pictures for her magazine texts. Together we hope that our combined efforts in this book of the Norfolk coastline proves entertaining and informative.

All royalties from this and subsequent books, as well as those from our previous book *Broads Eye View,* I intend to donate to charity.

Mike Page
Strumpshaw, Norfolk, Spring 2006

The Norfolk Coastline

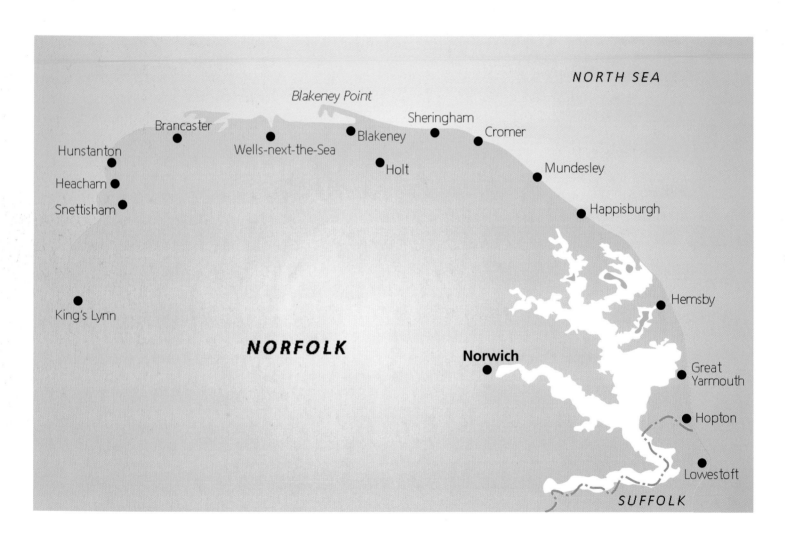

Hopton

Hopton marks the start of Norfolk although it hasn't always been so. Until the county boundaries were redrawn Hopton was in Suffolk. It was a small fishing village until the holiday industry arrived. Norfolk is largely an agricultural county as this view suggests. The steam plume from Cantley sugar beet processing factory is on the horizon.

Gorleston and Great Yarmouth

This high-level picture shows the distinctive curve of the Norfolk coastline and the expanse of Breydon Water. The recently built Scroby Sands windfarm and the planned new Great Yarmouth harbour just to the north of the existing harbour entrance is changing the landscape yet again.

Opposite: **Gorleston looking north-east**

Gorleston Pier

Old Gorleston sits on the rising land beyond the pier where the fishermen's cottages begin. The Pier itself used to house a lighthouse, the later red brick tower (1877) at the bend in the river replaced it but is no longer operating. The Lifeboat House used to be on the pier also but the lifeboat is now upriver of the old tower lighthouse. The red brick Pier Hotel (formerly the 'Hope & Anchor' – a pub frequented by beachmen & fishermen) and the white stuccoed Ocean Rooms (formerly the Floral Hall) stand opposite an 'Arts & Crafts' architectural gem – The Pavilion. This ornate building, sometime theatre sometime music hall, with terra cotta decorative bricks, four copper domes and Venetian tracery windows, was built in 1898 and is worth a special trip to Gorleston just for the visual pleasure found walking round the outside of the building. On the green at Brush Bend (aka Brush Quay) opposite the Pier Hotel stands a recently erected (2005) memorial commemorating the 60th anniversary of the Air Sea Rescue Service. At maximum strength in 1943–44, fourteen ASR boats operated out of Gorleston. Brush Bend allegedly takes its name from the quantities of brushwood used in the construction of the quay. The brushwood was washed in on the tides, collected, put into place, and weighted down with stones to consolidate it before repeating the process.

Yarmouth Harbour

Great Yarmouth already was a prosperous town when Horatio Nelson returned in triumph after the Battle of the Nile (1800), and from where he sailed to join the Fleet anchored in the Yarmouth Roads before the victorious Battle of Copenhagen (1801). The 'Finest Quay in all Europe' (Daniel Defoe 1784) contains elegant houses belonging originally to local merchants whose ships tied up alongside the quay. Yarmouth became famous for herring fishing and at the turn of the last century it was claimed that when the boats were tied up in the river it was possible to walk from bank to bank across their decks. Recently the town's prosperity came from vessels servicing the oil and gas industry. The new Yarmouth power station (centre) runs on North Sea gas. The South Denes spit of land has variously contained a race-course and an airstrip but today has a somewhat neglected appearance. Hopefully all that will change when the new Great Yarmouth harbour is built. The building on the southern pier of the harbour entrance is the former Coastguard Station, now housing Coastwatch. The sandy bay just past the harbour entrance on the right is the Spending Beach on to which ships in urgent need of repair can run.

The Golden Mile looking south

The Golden Mile contains all the usual seaside attractions including the Britannia and Wellington Piers and a fishing jetty. Near the power station stands Nelson's column, one hundred and forty four feet high, Yarmouth's tribute to Norfolk's famous son. Erected in 1817 (twenty-three years before its better known counterpart in Trafalgar Square) the plinth lists Nelson's victories whilst Britannia stands triumphant on the top. She is facing inland because (it has been claimed) Yarmouth's prosperity came from the river rather than from the sea. We wonder what Nelson would have said about that! Maybe she is facing the county of his birth. As part of the Trafalgar bicentenary the monument has been restored. On the North Denes (foreground) grows marram grass which counters wind erosion. Each May the RSPB cordons off an area to protect the nesting Little Tern.

Opposite: Yarmouth looking south

The Rivers Bure (near picture) and Yare meet in Yarmouth harbour just south of the Breydon Bridge. Installed in 1985 it has the largest lifting section of any bridge in Britain. Yarmouth racecourse is in the foreground. The promontory in the distance is Lowestoft's Ness Point, the most easterly part of Britain.

Great Yarmouth looking East

Centre is the largest parish church in England (green roof) part destroyed by enemy bombing 1942 and mainly rebuilt but minus its steeple. For centuries the steeple had been used as a landmark by passing ships. The Breydon (left) and Haven Bridges are the only road crossings downstream of the Norwich southern bypass bridge. The area of Cobholm (near centre) was very badly flooded in 1953. At Yarmouth Haven the River Bure flows into the Yare and so out to sea; the high building on the river houses the Coastguard headquarters. When the Romans manned their fort at Burgh Castle and their town at Caister, the site of what was to become Yarmouth was still under the sea but gradually a sandbank formed and a settlement developed in the tenth or eleventh centuries. Because of the flat Broadland terrain, Scroby Sands windfarm can be seen for miles inland.

North Denes
Here we are closer to the coast of Holland than we are to London.

Jumping Jack installation barge

Seen here entering Yarmouth harbour during the Scroby Sands wind turbine installation programme, 'Jumping Jack' has a 1200 tonnes capacity crane and a stable platform supporting offshore lifting and installation. The platform legs are jacked up by hydraulic winches and the whole was designed for repeated rig moves hence its name.

**MV *Ocean Ady* erecting a wind turbine base
on Scroby Sands 2003**

MV *Ocean Ady* and its sister craft MV *Ocean Hanne* are operated
by a Danish company specialising in wind turbine erection in
shallow waters. The *Ocean Ady* has four tension legs for stability
when operating the main lattice boom crane and two container
handling cranes, which act as tailing cranes, when erecting the
tower, and as pre-assembly cranes for the rotor.

***Seacore Excalibur* at Scroby**

A floating drilling platform at work on Scroby. The sea at this point
was too shallow to enable a conventional vessel to be positioned.

Windfarm under construction

There are thirty turbines standing 60 metres above sea level and piled up to 30 metres into the sea bed. Commissioned by Powergen Renewables Offshore each turbine has three 40m blades. In 2004 the power was brought onshore at North Denes where it was fed into the National Grid supplying 41000 homes with electricity.

Opposite: **Windfarm almost complete**

At low tide when most of the sands are uncovered, seals in their hundreds bask here. Boat trips out to the turbines have become a tourist attraction.

Caister looking North

Apart from a few cottages there's very little evidence now that Caister was once a prosperous fishing village and, earlier still, a Roman town. The very first holiday camp in Britain was created here at the turn of the last century and so began the holiday camps and caravan parks which run northwards along the coast as far as Sheringham. The wind turbines at Somerton are on the horizon.

Caister hazy days

The bright red building (foreground) is the Caister lifeboat shed. In the cemetery there's a touching marble memorial to the men of the *Beauchamp* lifeboat who were trapped when their boat overturned attempting a rescue in angry seas on November 13 1901. From an eye witness account of the incident has come their motto 'Caistermen never turn back'.

Caister's new lifeboat

The *Bernard Matthews II*, launched in July 2005, continues a long tradition of saving lives from this treacherous sandbank-laden part of the North Sea. Originally operated by the Beach Companies the RNLI took over the running of the Caister lifeboat from 1845 but withdrew in 1969. The Caister Volunteer Rescue Service has continued to this day and its previous boat the *Bernard Matthews* saved 105 lives. The new boat, a Dutch Valentijn Class, is the first offshore UK lifeboat to be powered by waterjet propulsion. With a top speed of 37 knots it cuts rescue time by two-thirds.

North Denes airfield

Originally a small grass airfield where holidaymakers could take joyrides over the Norfolk coast but now used only by helicopters servicing the North Sea oil industry. The busy coast road runs alongside.

California and Scratby

Crumbling cliffs run spasmodically from California all the way to Weybourne. The line of granite stones offers some protection from high waves. In the foreground is a curve marking the former track of the Yarmouth and Stalham Light Railway 1877 (later part of the M&GN). It ran from Yarmouth Beach Station to North Walsham and Melton Constable.

Below: **California and Scratby cliffs**

Probably as a result of a shipwreck, a number of sixteenth-century gold coins were found at the base of these cliffs in the 1840s. Possibly because this coincided with the California Gold Rush the lonely stretch of beach became Norfolk's own California.

Scratby cliffs

A Beach Company was formed in Scratby in 1842. Beach Companies existed all along the coast from Mundesley to Aldeburgh. Their primary purpose was to salvage whatever could be saved from boats in danger of sinking. But from these companies came the beginnings of the lifeboat movement for although the Beachmen were motivated by profit they came also to the rescue of sailors and fishermen. But from all accounts it was bounty first, rescue second!

Opposite: **California beach**
The beach access is protected.

Newport and Hemsby

Another colony of Beachmen was formed in the area they christened Newport, part of the parish of Hemsby. They built cottages and a beer-house called 'The Cottage on the Cliff'. Hemsby church sits in the middle of the village proper whilst the holiday industry seems within the last century to have taken over all the land eastwards to the beach.

Hemsby beach – summer

Hemsby beach – summer. Difficult to imagine now that this was once a quiet fishing village.

Right: **Hemsby – December**
Where have all the holidaymakers gone?

Winterton and The Ness

The sand dunes were planted with marram grass in the 1950s to slow down sand erosion. The beach has, over several hundred years, built into a Ness or point (from the French nez or nose). Winterton, until the decline of the fishing industry after the Second World War, had been the prime seafaring settlement along the east coast and had a tradition of providing coxswains for several of the neighbouring lifeboats. There were two lighthouses at the point in the nineteenth century.

Opposite: **Winterton looking north**

Winterton churchyard contains the graves of many shipwrecked sailors and some of the older houses are built from the timbers of wrecked ships. The holiday chalets have been arranged in zig-zag lines and random groups in an attempt to create a bit of variety and privacy.

Winterton October 2002

Winterton October 2004

Compare these two pictures taken two years apart to see how destructive the sea can be!

Winterton beach
The houses lie low behind the dunes but the wind turbines at West Somerton dominate the landscape.

Winterton Ness

Opposite: **The original mouth of the River Thurne**

The Thurne would have flowed into a large estuary on this spot at Horsey but its mouth became blocked by a large sand spit, and by the Middle Ages the river had changed direction flowing westwards into the River Bure as it does today. Its dried up course can be picked out north of Martham Broad then, as a meander towards the coast, along the Hundred Stream. The dark circle foreground is a water-filled depression on a reserve owned by the Norfolk Wildlife Trust. Horsey Mere is in the foreground with Heigham Sound and the large expanse of Hickling Broad top of picture.

Horsey beach regeneration

Horsey is the area of the coast most at risk from tidal surges. If the sea broke through again as it did most recently in 1897, 1938 and 1953 a large part of northern Broadland would be under salt water with the accompanying destruction of plant and animal life. In 1784 the curate of Horsey, on his journey from Winterton, complained that several times he had narrowly escaped drowning.

Sand pumping off Horsey

Horsey beach is being reinforced with sand dredged by the Dutch vessel *Geopotes 15* from half a mile out to sea.

Horsey grey seals
Who's looking at who?

Horsey low tide
Breakwater repair and replacement.

37

Waxham
Several hundred years ago the village of Waxham Parva was lost to the sea, the fate over the centuries of several villages along this part of the East coast. The church is in Waxham Magna now known simply as Waxham.

Opposite: **Horsey looking south**
The proximity of The Broads and their vulnerability clearly can be seen. Horsey Mere is foreground with the non navigable Blackfleet Broad close by (top left). Hickling Broad is off to the right and the divided Martham Broad is left. The Trinity Broads are in the near distance whilst the long muddy expanse of Breydon Water shows up on the skyline.

Waxham Great Barn

At 180 feet this is one of the longest barns in the county and certainly the oldest. Built around 1580 by Thomas Woodhouse with brick, flint and limestone plundered from abandoned monastic buildings, it served as the granary for his large estate. By 1987 it had become derelict even before a gale took most of the roof off. It has been restored by Norfolk County Council and English Heritage together and is open during the summer months.

Opposite: **Waxham and Sea Palling winter storms**

In this winter picture the force of the angry sea has been diminished by the groups of boulders imported from Scandinavia to form nine, 42 metre long reefs. A Dutch company specialising in flood defence engineering carried out the work 1993–97 for the Environment Agency. The boulders' life expectancy is 50 years. Since their installation there has been no erosion or serious flooding at this point.

Sea Palling reefs
The reefs newly installed. Compare this with the previous picture!

Sea Palling beach
The beach has built up behind the reefs creating a playground.

Jet ski charity event

The first 'hundred by hundred by hundred' event took place in 2001. The skiers each paid £100 to enter, a hundred jet skiers took part and the event covered 100km. It was the brainchild of the Deary family of Sea Palling who have a business selling jet skis. The course, with safety backup, ran from Sea Palling to Great Yarmouth where participants were met by the Mayor, back to Sea Palling for lunch then up to Cromer to be received by the Chairman of North Norfolk District Council. The idea was to raise money for charity. The Variety Club of Great Britain, Big C Cancer and the Blind/Deaf Charities all benefited. £25000 was raised in the three years the event ran and it's hoped to start it up again in a couple of years.

Opposite: **Sea Palling surf**
Surfers surf safely within the lagoons created by the reefs.

Opposite: **Eccles Bush estate in winter**

The pre-war Bush Estate consists of small bungalows, many of them holiday homes. They lie behind the Dunes. As early as 1933 the North Rivers Catchment Board warned the developers of the dangers of flooding.

Eccles looking north

'Eccles by the Sea is a decayed parish, once a noted fishing town with a lordship of 2000 acres but so wasted by the ocean that the inhabitants in their petition for a reduction of taxes in 1605 complained that they had only 14 houses and 300 acres of land the rest being all destroyed by the sea'. And this was written 150 years ago! The sea continued to destroy the village so that by 1900 all that was left was the church tower rising out of the beach and now that too is gone. No longer Eccles by the Sea but Eccles in the Sea.

Cart Gap
Because there are no natural harbours along this stretch of coastline, gaps were driven through the dunes enabling fishermen to drag their boats down to the water.

Happisburgh in peril
Happisburgh has been affected more badly by recent cliff erosion than any other village along this part of the coast. The breakwaters erected in the 1950s are breaking up, the village is unprotected and erosion is happening at an increasing pace.

Happisburgh SOS

Villagers are seeking as much publicity as possible for urgent Government action to slow erosion. And at present there's no Government compensation for houses lost to the sea. On 27 August 2003 they gathered to spell out their message in dramatic form.

Happisburgh 1996
Going…

Happisburgh October 2004
going…

Opposite: **Happisburgh October 2005**
almost gone.

Ostend new housing development
Despite coastal erosion houses continue to be built in vulnerable places.

Opposite: **Happisburgh lighthouse**
Following a disastrous storm on 30 October 1789 in which eighty fishing boats were lost between Yarmouth and Cromer, and one hundred and twenty dead bodies were washed up on to the beach, Trinity House decided to build a lighthouse at Happisburgh. Two coastguard cottages, now privately owned, surround it. The two low, square structures in the fields are wartime pillboxes.

Walcott Gap and Bacton
When the seas are very rough the police close this stretch of road.

Keswick and Bacton

There's quite a lot of history in this picture! Bromholme Priory (the ruins to the left of the houses) was founded in 1113, then came Bacton church c.1400 followed by the village houses built from the late nineteenth century onwards, and finally Bacton gas terminal begun in 1968.

Walcot, Keswick and Bacton

Walcot and Keswick are all that are left of villages claimed by the sea. Bacton was described by Nikolaus Pevsner (*The Buildings of England*) as 'one of the prettiest in this part of Norfolk' but that was before the gas terminal was built!

Opposite: **Bromholme, Broomholm or Bromholm Priory**

Founded by Cluniac Monks in 1113 as a cell to Castle Acre, the fortunes of the Priory improved considerably in 1223 when it was claimed to possess a piece of the True Cross. Visitors flocked; the Norfolk coast always has attracted visitors including the pilgrims in Chaucer's *Canterbury Tales* and *Piers Plowman* the subject of William Langland's (c.1330) poem who says 'Bid the rood (cross) of Bromholm bring me out of debt'! At the Dissolution of the Monasteries by Henry V111 (1536) the Priory was abandoned.

Opposite: **Bacton Village**

Bacton Terminal

Gas first came ashore here in 1968 from the Leman Field, the then largest known gas field in the world. Gas is also piped abroad. The fields in current production are connected to Bacton by SEAL pipeline, 474 km of it, from the Shearwater and Elgin Fields. The complex to the left of picture is the Interconnector Terminal sending gas to the continent.

Bacton Terminal looking south

Mundesley low level

The coming of the railway brought the holiday industry with it and changed this Norfolk fishing village into a resort. Hotels and convalescent homes appeared so that their clientele could benefit from the bracing Norfolk air. There's no longer a lifeboat stationed at Mundesley but there is an Inshore Rescue Boat and Coastwatch occupy the square red brick building on The Green. The 'golf ball' of RAF Trimingham's radar station is on the horizon.

Right: **Mundesley high level**

Mundesley

Mundesley lies on either side of the valley of the diminutive River Mun from which it takes its name.

**Mundesley
breakwater repairs**

Clifftop caravan sites

Trimingham Radome
Whilst Mundesley's Coastwatch organisation keeps watch over the sea, RAF Trimingham's radar dome keeps watch over the skies.

Right: **Trimingham**
These are the highest cliffs along the Norfolk coast.

Sidestrand cliff fall

Cliff falls here are nothing new. In 1881 most of the clifftop church was moved stone-by-stone a third of a mile inland because it had begun to fall down the cliff.

Overstrand looking south-east

Longshore drift is the movement of beach material. Here the sea is washing into the cliff and carrying material northwards on the ebb tide.

Opposite: **Overstrand**

In the 1890s Overstrand could be said to 'have arrived'. Wealthy people built holiday homes here, most notably The Pleasaunce designed by Edwin Lutyens for Lord Battersea, and Overstrand Hall, again by Lutyens, for banker Lord Hillingdon. The village today retains the feel of a quiet and prosperous seaside village but a sombre note is introduced by the abrupt finish to the High Street – tumbled down the cliff.

Overstrand looking towards Cromer
Cromer lighthouse (still working) with Beeston Bump on the horizon. The bright canopies of hang gliders can just be seen in the distance. Copying the seagulls they're taking advantage of the thermal lift from the cliffs. This view of Cromer is the one most often appearing on 1930s railway posters.

Opposite: **Overstrand looking North west**
There are several Norfolk golf courses sited right at the coast's edge. As the cliffs erode the courses get smaller!

Cromer international airport
Sited at Northrepps this small grass strip really is international. Light aircraft fly in from the continent

Opposite: **Cromer cliffs towards the town**

Cromer

Cromer was just another fishing village clustered around the church until it was discovered as a resort. There's a wealth of elegant Georgian and Victorian buildings along the seafront. A regeneration scheme, part funded by the EU, has provided a new Lifeboat Museum, seafront enhancement and town centre revitalisation all of which are aimed to attract visitors together with learning and community facilities for residents.

Cromer seafront

Architect George Skipper's 1895 Hotel de Paris, originally Lord Suffield's summer residence, has a prime site standing high and opposite the pier. As with all seaside places between Great Yarmouth and Blakeney, Cromer has no harbour. The crab boats have to be pulled up on to the beach. Cromer lifeboat in its shed on the end of the Pier has a long history of courageous rescues. Cromer's most famous son is Henry Blogg (1876–1954), lifeboatman for fifty-three years and coxswain for thirty-eight of them. He remains the most highly decorated lifeboatman ever. Among his awards were the George Cross and British Empire Medal. During his tenure the Cromer lifeboat is recorded as having saved 873 lives.

Cromer seagull's eye view

The church tower at 160 feet is the highest in Norfolk. For centuries it has been a landmark from the sea although the sea is closer to it now than it used to be. Shipden, three miles out, is yet another village that has been lost to the sea. The present pier is 151 metres long, the third on the site and the second to be sliced in two! In 1897 a coal barge collided with it and in 1993 a runaway oil barge cut it in two. During the Second World War it was sectioned to prevent enemy landings.

Opposite: **Cromer looking south-east**

Cromer from overhead Roman Camp
At 329 feet, Roman Camp is the lowest high point of any county. Nor has the camp anything to do with the Romans. Iron Age workings have been found here.

Opposite: **East Runton**
East and West Runton – two villages but only one parish and one church.

West Runton beach

In 1991 beach walkers discovered some very large bones at the foot of the cliff. They turned out to be Britain's oldest fossil, part of the skeleton of a prehistoric elephant. It's thought that the 10 tonne mammal, as high as a double decker bus, had become trapped in what was then a swamp 600000 years ago. The bones of the 'Runton Elephant' are in the Norwich Castle Museum for further study and reconstruction and are on display until 2007.

This is the only place in Norfolk where genuine rock pools are to be found. The pools are in a chalk layer surrounded by flint edges thus preventing fish, sea anemones, molluscs and seaweeds from being washed away with the tides.

Beeston Bump

There's a 63 metre triangulation point near the top of the mound. Beeston Hill's silhouette looks even more dramatic from the coast road on its opposite side. The Norfolk Long Distance Coast Path runs across the top.

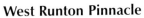

West Runton Pinnacle

Nicknamed 'The Pinnacle' by locals, the column broke away from the cliff several years ago. Each year it loses height as storms take their toll and as high winter tides wash round the base it becomes more isolated from the rest of the cliff. The white chalk strata have flint particles dotted through them.

Sheringham beach

Like Cromer, Sheringham has no natural harbour so the crab boats are pulled up on to The Driftway next to the old Lifeboat Station. The *Henry Ramey Upcher,* which saw service 1894–1935, had sixteen oars, sails and a crew of nineteen. In bad weather there were two men at each oar so the boat contained a total crew of thirty-five even before beginning the rescue! The old town is grouped round the beach. By its rivals in Cromer, the inhabitants used to be referred to deprecatingly as 'Shannocks' from the dialect 'shanny' or 'shaddock' meaning rowdy.

Sheringham: Home of the North Norfolk Railway

'The Poppy Line', staffed almost entirely by volunteers, runs on the old M&GN track between Sheringham and Holt. Rolling stock of historic interest is hauled by locomotives which ran originally on many different parts of the railway system. The stations (Sheringham, Weybourne, Kelling Heath and Holt) and station furnishings along the 5½ mile route are the originals or replicas of the buildings and equipment of the M&GN era. Sheringham Station (1887) has quaint period features such as Victorian ironwork, a vintage booking hall and a ladies' waiting room with the original fireplace. In the near future it's hoped to reinstate the level crossing and join the line once more to the national rail network.

Sheringham

The stone War Memorial (centre) in Sheringham's residential area is fenced by a low railing of metalworked poppies. This is doubly appropriate because not only is Sheringham part of 'Poppyland' but British Legion poppy wreaths are laid there each November on Remembrance Day. Poppyland was a term coined by London theatre critic Clement Scott who 'discovered' the Cromer and Sheringham area and in 1883 wrote a *Daily Telegraph* article in extolling its qualities. This lead to the hordes of visitors who continue to this day. Scott subsequently was recorded as having regretted writing the article.

Sheringham autumn colours

Autumn colours of the trees on National Trust land outside Sheringham. Iron Age workings have been found here. 'Beeston Bump' is profiled on the skyline.

Opposite: **Sheringham and Beeston Regis**

Sheringham looking towards Cromer. The rectangle near foreground is a model boat pond.

'Green Arrow' between Sheringham and Weybourne
Steam locomotive 'Green Arrow' on loan 2004 to the North Norfolk Railway (The Poppy Line) from the National Railway Museum, York. The 2-6-2 Gresley V2 Class engine, built 1936, was operated by the LNER.

'Green Arrow' approaching Weybourne
Resembling more a 1930s railway poster than a high tech digital aerial photograph, 'Green Arrow' puffs its way across the beautiful North Norfolk countryside with Weybourne Mill and the coast in the background.

Weybourne

'He who would England win must first at Weybourne Hope begin'. The beach slopes steeply allowing ships to get close to the shore. Elizabeth I made elaborate defences against invasion here by the Spanish Armada, and in the First World War troops embarked for France from Weybourne beach. During the Second World War modified Tiger Moth aircraft ('Queen Bees') without pilots and flown by radio control were launched by catapult and for a while used for target practice. Winston Churchill came to witness the exercise. The Muckleburgh Collection of military memorabilia is housed on the former Army Camp (top of picture). A small landing strip makes the site a popular summer venue for light aircraft.

Weybourne Mill

John Dawson is listed as Weybourne Mill's first owner in 1845. In 1859 and 1860 he advertised for a tenant. By 1869 he was bankrupt and the following appeared in the *Norfolk News* 28 May 1870:

> TO LET at WEYBOURNE near Holt.
> A first class tower windmill driving three pairs of stones with Miller's house attached.
> Also 5 acres of good land with the prospect of hiring 40 or 50 acres more
> to parties that can give good reference as to character and capital.
> Immediate possession may be had of the mill, the land at Michaelmas next.

Salthouse looking towards Blakeney

There is thought to have been a salt warehouse (from which the place takes its name) here as early as the eleventh century. Although the village has been landlocked since 1638 previously it had a thriving salt fish industry. Cod and herring boats sailed as far as Iceland from the several small, now silted up, ports along this stretch of coast. The shingle bank beyond the marshes has been breached on more than one occasion. This part of the coast always has been victim of 'Rages' (tidal storms), the Great Rages of 1861 and 1897 and the 1953 floods being three of the most damaging. Saltmarshes begin to form where the sea is shallow. When a spit occurs they're protected from the sea. Mud and finer sediments settle out of the water initially forming mud flats. In time vegetation grows and stabilises the marsh. Saltmarshes and their fronting mud flats are the only natural wilderness areas left in the UK.

Opposite: **Salthouse**

Salthouse Church stands high above the marshes out of flood danger. In the choir stalls there's seventeenth century graffiti in the form of crudely scratched sailing vessels.

Salthouse shingle bank

The Norfolk Coast Path is on the shingle bank which makes for hard walking. The pools of Cley Marshes Nature Reserve are in the distance. There's an unbroken chain of Nature Reserves from Weybourne to Holme near Hunstanton. The Salthouse bank peters out at Cley.

Cley looking towards Blakeney Point

From Cley Mill there's a magnificent view across the marshes to Blakeney Point. Cley Mill, now a guest house, was grinding corn until the end of the First World War.

Cley and Wiveton looking North

Wiveton (left) and Cley churches face one another across the Glaven Valley. It's alleged that the builders of Wiveton Church put their richest flint flushwork on the side facing Cley so as to impress the Cley parishioners. But Norfolk people don't impress that easily! The valley was once a river estuary used by the Glaven ports of Cley, Wiveton and Blakeney. There are marks on the churchyard wall where ships once tied up. The original Cley village was centered around the church but a major fire in the seventeenth century destroyed many houses and most of the village moved down closer to the water.

River Glaven diversion

On a short stretch of river near the shingle ridge, the River Glaven is being diverted to give flood protection in the Glaven Valley. The mouth of the river is being moved westwards. The spoil is being used to fill in the earlier river bed. Man-made intervention on the saltmarshes is nothing new. The whole area is wildife rich and the Environment Agency is taking measures to keep disturbance to a minimum. The brown scar denotes the work under way, the old river mouth (right of picture) will be filled in with the excavated material.

Cley

The village was cut off permanently from the sea in the seventeenth century when land was reclaimed and embankments were built. Along this part of the coast it's Cley which suffers first when big tidal surges occur. A Dutch influence exists in some of the older buildings and there is an eighteenth century Custom House. In the thirteenth century Cley had ranked fourth in the list of England's top ports, and in its heyday wool was shipped from Cley to the Low Countries.

Norfolk Wildlife Trust's Cley Reserve

Today Cley is the nerve centre of the nation's 'twitchers' who flock year round to see the abundance and diversity of migratory and resident birds. Cley was the first Norfolk Naturalist Trust's Reserve (now the Norfolk Wildlife Trust) and was set up in 1926.

Opposite: **Blakeney looking West**

Blakeney was at one time sited inland, the coastal village of Snitterley has washed away into the North Sea. Unusually Blakeney's church has a tower at either end. The taller, at 104 feet, served as a landmark, the second tower may have housed a beacon. When the Armada threatened, thirty-six boats were sent from Blakeney, Wiveton and Cley. Because the area is so popular with second-home owners and the consequent high property prices, the Blakeney Housing Society came into being to provide cottages for local people. A blue plaque identifies those dwellings. On the skyline: the tip of Blakeney Point to the right, Stiffkey and Wells approach to the left with Holkham Meals in the far distance.

Blakeney looking east
Mercifully the busy coast road by-passes some of the village.

Opposite: **Blakeney from the Quay**
Blakeney boats were present at the siege of Calais 1347 and in the reign of Elizabeth I ships from the three Glaven ports went as far as Iceland fishing for cod. But because of marsh enclosures the harbour has silted up and today only small sailing boats and the trip boats, going out to see the seals on Blakeney Point, can get in and out, and even their movements are governed by the tide. Blakeney has been victim of severe flooding over the centuries as marker plaques on the quay show and even today the flood siren stands in the village ready for use.

Blakeney lifeboat house

Now a biology field base for University College London and also an Information Centre, the Lifeboat Station closed in 1935 but had been active from 1823 when The Norfolk Association for Saving the Lives of Shipwrecked Mariners had decided to install lifeboats at Yarmouth, Winterton, Blakeney, Burnham Overy or Brancaster and Hunstanton.

Opposite: **Blakeney Point**

The point is a shingle spit with a long bank of sand whose material gradually, by wave action, is being moved westwards along the coast. It's estimated that Blakeney Point has doubled in length over the last thousand years. It's one of the few places in the country where shingle bank, sand dunes and saltmarsh occur together. It was Norfolk's first Nature Reserve and became part of the National Trust in 1912. Access is on foot along the beach from Cley or by boat from Morston or Blakeney quays.

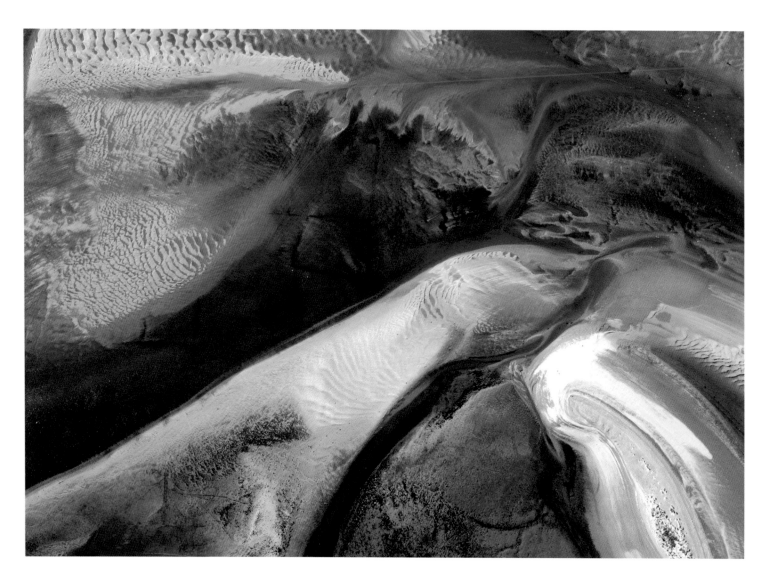

Blakeney Point at low tide

Blakeney Point at high tide

Blakeney Point sunset

Opposite: **Blakeney Point seals**

There's a colony of an estimated five hundred common and grey seals living here year round. A popular trip especially in the warmer months is to take an hour-long boat trip to the Point from Morston or Blakeney quays. Most numerous are the silver grey to brown common seals; the grey seals are darker with heavy blotchy coats and larger heads.

Morston

Morston marshes are part of the Blakeney National Trust Nature Reserve. On the quay there are Information and observation rooms for watching the many species of sea birds, among them Terns (Little, Common, Sandwich and Arctic), Ringed Plovers, Oystercatchers and Shelduck. One of the Blakeney Point ferries departs from the quay. Samphire grows here on Morston Marshes and is harvested in the summer months. It's an acquired taste.

Left: **Stiffkey**

The River Stiffkey winds round the village to marshes which are part of yet another silted up harbour. 'Stewkey blues' were cockles gathered for centuries by the women of the village until the 1950s. One of Stiffkey's residents found fame whilst another found notoriety. Henry Williamson (1895–1977), author of *Tarka the Otter* (on which the film 'Ring of Bright Water' was based) lived in the village; a blue plaque marks his house. A Rector of Stiffkey, the Reverend Harold Davidson, because of his association with London prostitutes, in 1932 was tried in a court of law then unfrocked in Norwich Cathedral. He protested his innocence but ended his days in a travelling circus preaching the Gospel from inside an (already occupied) lion's cage. The lion mauled him to death which suggests that his judgement in more than one matter was not entirely sound.

Stiffkey Hall and Church

The present church is dedicated to St John the Baptist whose head became a trophy for those wanting revenge, much as the Reverend Davidson's did six centuries later. In the churchyard stand the ruins of another church, St Mary's. The remains of Stiffkey Hall c.1550 include the towers, part of the house, the gatehouse and the ruins of the Great Hall. Built by Nathaniel Bacon, whose father was Keeper of the Great Seal, the house originally was U-shaped with four corner towers and other towers within the fabric.

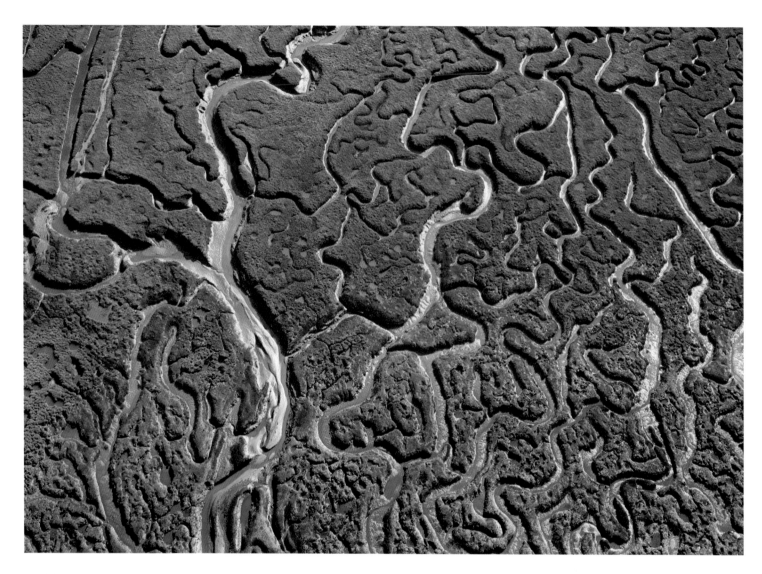

Stiffkey Marsh patterns winter

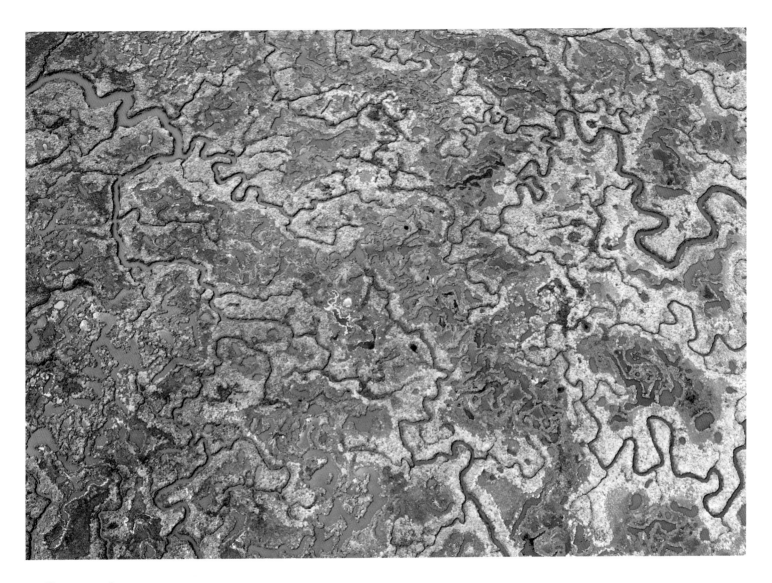

Stiffkey Marsh patterns summer

Harbour approach and East Hills

No picture could better demonstrate the trickiness of getting into Wells Harbour! And to complete the challenge there's a sand bar at the entrance. Cockle Hole is to the west, Bob Hall's Sand to the east. It's advisable to use the channel pilot. Brent Geese feed on the mud flats of East Hills.

Opposite: **Coast panorama**

East Hills and Wells harbour, the pines of Holkham Meals, Burnham Overy Creek, Scolt Head with Thornham on the horizon.

Wells Harbour

For larger boats this is the only harbour northwards from Great Yarmouth. Until recently grain, fertiliser, coal and animal feed were brought in or taken out by coasters tied up alongside the Quay. But no longer, now even the prominent Granary has been converted to housing. The Wells Harbour Project begun in 2004 aims to rejuvenate the area including restoration of the old Lifeboat House near the Quay and provide better facilities and easier access for visiting boats. Stonemeal Creek and other channels through the marshes are suitable for exploration only by canoe.

Albatros off Wells

This Dutch 1899 Rotterdam-built sailing barge is one of the oldest sailing ships still afloat. Her owner/skipper Tom Brouwer acquired her in 1980 and until 1996 she carried soya bean meal into Wells from Belgium, after which she was working out of Dutch ports for Greenpeace. When the Greenpeace contract ended in 2000 her owner began a corporate hospitality package, joined in 2001 by *Albatros* becoming also an Education Centre and giving sea trips, sail training and related activities so as to remain commercially viable. Having a deeper draught than an inshore barge, operating in and out of Wells harbour can be a challenge. Several times she has run aground but refloats again with a high tide. But in May 2002 *Albatros* ran aground somewhat dramatically and stuck in the harbour mud for three weeks until a Dutch Company used hawsers to pull her off.

Wells

Distinctly different terrain on either side of the channel. To the east is natural saltmarsh, to the west and bounded by a sea wall is land drained by an Earl of Leicester in the middle of the nineteenth century. The pines in the background were planted at the same time in a bid to slow wind erosion. The churchyard (centre) contains the grave of John Fryer, master of the *Bounty* until Fletcher Christian was promoted over his head.

Wells Harbour channel low tide

The entrance channel is 'The Run' leading to 'The Pool' near the quay. In 1800 the port was so busy that twelve pilots were employed. The red-roofed Lifeboat Shed has been there since 1898, previously from 1830 it was on the quay in what is now the Harbour Commissioner's Office and Wells Maritime Museum. The service was run first by the Norfolk Shipwreck Association then from 1869 by the RNLI. Today the building houses both an Inshore and an All Weather Lifeboat.

A distinguised visitor to Wells

The royal yacht *Britannia* anchored off Wells during the summer of 1996.

Wells looking towards Blakeney

At the junction of the Quay and Beach Road is a touching memorial to most of the crew of the *Eliza Adams* lifeboat. The 1880 disaster left ten widows and twenty-seven orphans.

Holkham Hall

Thomas Coke, First Earl of Leicester, began Holkham Hall in 1734. The architects were William Kent and Norwich's Matthew Brettingham; the style Palladian. Capability Brown designed the parkland. The lake is the remnant of the original saltwater creek, there before the land was drained. Coke's (pronounced 'Cook') great nephew, heir and namesake was 'Coke of Norfolk' agricultural reformer. The eighty feet high obelisk in the parkland was commissioned by his tenants and bears carvings of farm animals and wheatsheaves.

Opposite: **Holkham pines**

The beach is the one (supposedly Bermuda) over which Gwyneth Paltrow walked in the closing scenes of 'Shakespeare in Love' 1998. The several varieties of pines have been there rather longer. Planted in the 1860s to protect the reclaimed land from erosion in Autumn, the trees are an important landfall site for rare species of migrating birds. And there's a resident population of breeding Crossbills.

Burnham Overy Staithe looking west
The land rises steeply (steeply for Norfolk that is) to the south-west, and the windmill, which dates from 1814, stands sixty feet above sea level.

Opposite: **Burnham Overy Staithe looking east**
'Staithe' – comes from the Old English 'landing place'. Burnham Overy Staithe was once a busy port. The harbour looks across to Scolt Head. There are conflicting opinions about where Horatio Nelson learned to sail (some say Barton Broad) but it's possible that in Burnham Creek he first took the helm, since he was born only a couple of miles away at Burnham Thorpe.

Burnham Thorpe: Nelson's birthplace

Nelson's father was Rector here at the time of his famous son's birth 1758. Horatio was the sixth of eleven children. The Rectory no longer stands but the church contains much Nelson memorabilia.

Left: **Burnham Market**

The largest of the seven Burnhams and the site of a mediaeval market for the surrounding area, hence the name. The presence of the market gave rise to a distinctly urban community. Because today of its popularity with rich people from London the village has been nicknamed 'Burnham Upmarket'.

Burnham Norton

There are seven Burnhams in north-west Norfolk. Nikolaus Pevsner, cataloguer of the significant buildings of England, explains the cluster of Burnham villages as due to the area's mediaeval prosperity. Each Burnham is within a mile of its neighbour and each has its own church.

Scolt Head high tide

The sandhills of Scolt Head are thought to resemble ringworm on a skull /scolt. The island is 4 miles long and 1 mile wide covering 1620 acres. The National Trust and Norfolk Wildlife Trust own the island jointly. There's a large ternery (Sandwich Terns) in the summer, and year-round residents include Oystercatchers and Redshank, whilst Widgeon, Brent Geese and Pink Footed Geese are winter visitors. During World War Two, locals collected Tern eggs for food.

Scolt Head low tide

Brancaster Staithe and Brancaster
The two clusters are a mile apart. Brancaster Staithe has the harbour, Brancaster the church and the site of the Roman fort, *Branodunum*.

Opposite: **Brancaster Staithe**
Paradise for sailors, Mow Creek in the foreground; the western end of Scolt Head on the horizon.

Titchwell Village

Titchwell has just a cluster of houses and is best known for the RSPB Reserve on the marshes. The church has the round tower typical of so many Norfolk churches. The reason for this is that flint is the local material and it's difficult to make corners with flint. Richer churches imported stone to deal with the problem. In the nineteenth century the seven-hundred-year-old font was discovered in a field being used as a drinking trough!

Opposite: **Brancaster Staithe looking south-east**
The Norfolk Coast path lies between the houses and the saltmarshes.

Titchwell RSPB Reserve

The marshes were farmland until the 1953 floods destroyed the 1780s sea wall. In 1973 the RSPB bought 420 acres and leased the fore-shore. Rich habitats abound in the tidal and freshwater reed beds, salt and freshwater marshes. The success of the Reserve is demonstrated by the large numbers and varied species which are to be seen here. It's a winter roost for Hen Harriers, Marsh Harriers and last year there were 30 Little Egrets. Alec Watson tells of Sammy, a Black Winged Stilt, who first appeared in 1993 but has not been seen since mid 2005. It is thought he might have died or become victim of a predator.

Opposite: **Titchwell RSPB Reserve looking south**

NWT Holme

The coast begins the gradual curve towards The Wash. Norfolk Wildlife Trust's Holme Dunes Reserve is one of the closest landfalls for wintering birds from the Arctic and Greenland. The site has a number of designations among which are SSSI and Wetland of International Importance under the Ramsar Convention. The natterjack toad wouldn't be aware of these august titles but chooses this place as one of its habitats. Corsican pines were planted nearly a century ago to stabilise the dunes and more than 300 species of birds have been recorded.

Opposite: **Thornham**

Ship Lane, Staithe Lane and The Lifeboat pub all give clues to the fact that Thornham was once a port. Coal came in and grain went out but the railways took away the trade, the last granary was demolished by the 1953 floods. There's no land between here and the North Pole.

Holme Sea Henge

The timber circle on the beach between the high and low water marks was discovered in January 1999. Its significance is not entirely understood but the henge is believed to have been part of a Bronze Age ritual. Built in the same period as Stonehenge it was in place for approximately 4000 years. Because the lower timbers were in marshy peat they survived. But as the timbers became uncovered they started to dry out and eventually would have disintegrated completely. They were removed first to the Bronze Age Centre at Flag Fen, Peterborough, and subsequently to the Mary Rose Trust at Portsmouth where they are undergoing conservation. It's hoped to begin returning the timbers to Norfolk in 2007 where they will be on display at Lynn Museum. When the henge was revealed at Holme, visitors (human) created a conflict with visitors (winter migrant birds) which live or nest on the beach in the Reserve.

Holme Village
Here the ancient path of Peddars Way joins the recently created North Norfolk Coast Path so giving a continuous long distance walk from Ixworth in Suffolk to Cromer.

Old Hunstanton

Hunstanton, or Hunston, takes its name from the short River Hun which rises from springs in old Hunstanton Park, seat of the LeStrange family. Among the LeStrange family's titles are 'Lord High Admiral of the Wash', whose estates 'run down to the sea and beyond the tide-line as far as a man can ride on horseback and throw a javelin'. Hunstanton is the only East Coast resort facing west. The Lincolnshire coast is visible across The Wash.

Old Hunstanton

The old lighthouse became the Coastguard Station. This was one of the four oldest lighthouses in East Anglia (along with Winterton, Orford Ness and Harwich). The light was coal fired originally and burned down in 1777 being rebuilt by the Trinity Brethren. But the light was turned off for ever in 1921 and today the lighthouse is a private residence. The square red brick building to the left is used by Coastwatch.

Hunstanton Pier

There was a 'proper' seaside pier here in the 1890s, Victorian ladies walked along its windswept length to take the benefit of the bracing sea air. It was replaced by another pier in the 1930s but that was swept away in 1978. It might seem that Hunstanton piers are cursed. The present apology for a pier, pier only in that it was on the same site, no length to it at all, was burned down in 2002.

The area surrounding the green is the centre of New Hunstanton created as a seaside resort by the LeStrange family 1846. The resort's popularity was boosted both by royal patronage when Edward Prince of Wales (later Edward VII) convalesced here whilst recovering from typhoid and by the railway which arrived on 3 October 1862.

Opposite: **Hunstanton Cliffs**

The distinctive fossil rich cliffs consist of glacial deposits of white chalk, red ironstone and yellow carrstone, the latter is the local building material. The chalk is a seam which runs all the way from the Chilterns. To the right of the lighthouse stand the ruins of St Edmund's Chapel.

Heacham

Although caravans seem to take up half the village, the other half contains what was once a feudal village. It belonged to the Rolfe family. In 1614 John Rolfe of Heacham Hall, one of the early American colonists, married Pocahontas, daughter of a native American chief, and brought her to Heacham. Three years later as Sir Walter Raleigh set out on his last expedition to Virginia, Pocahontas died on board the ship en route to the place of her birth and is buried at Gravesend. On the edge of the village lies the Victorian Caley Mill famous for its Norfolk Lavender enterprise. A mill on the same site was mentioned in Domesday Book.

Opposite: **Hunstanton**

To the south the holiday industry has enlarged the town still further. The large car park (centre) is on the site of the railway station which closed in 1969. The path of the dismantled railway track is the straight line running between two caravan sites.

Sandringham

The estate was bought by Queen Victoria for the future Edward VII in 1861. Walter Rye, writing of the house in 1885 says:

'Sandringham itself is nothing to see. It was bought vastly dear and has had a tremendous lot of money spent on it and is still a very poor place for the heir apparent.'

The light soil and sandy heathland of the area gives rise to the description Sandy Dersingham (the next village) hence 'Sandringham'.

Wolferton Station

The King's Lynn to Hunstanton Railway opened in 1862. The station was created to enable the Royals or their visitors easily to reach Sandringham. On alighting from the train the party received refreshment (and other facilities) before continuing by coach to Sandringham House. Servants had to walk the two miles. Following the station's closure it was bought by the Sandringham Estate and became first a private house then a museum now closed.

Snettisham

In 1948 a plough unearthed Iron Age gold torcs (neck bands) and occasionally thereafter more treasure was dug up on site. But it wasn't until 1990 that five complete torcs in one Snettisham excavation were found by metal detection. The British Museum made further digs and discovered copper bracelets, coins and silver and gold torques. Norwich Castle Museum has examples on permanent display. It's possible that the objects were buried either for safe keeping or as part of a ritual. The Snettisham Treasure is considered to be the richest hoard in Britain. But the village has another treasure, the rare mediaeval church spire.

RSPB Reserve Snettisham

The waters of The Wash and the Reserve attract wading birds. At very high tides, waders are pushed from the mud flats of The Wash onto the Reserve and onto surrounding farmland. Pink Footed Geese, some forty thousand of them, arrive from Iceland for the winter and roost on the Reserve.

Opposite: **RSPB Reserve Snettisham low tide**

Kings Lynn looking north

Kings Lynn, known as Bishop's Lynn until 1536 when it was seized by King Henry VIII, has been a port since the Middle Ages. The docks in the picture were built more than a century and a half ago and today have bulk and container facilities to handle grain, timber, oil and wheat. A foot ferry operates across the tidal Great Ouse to West Lynn. Much of the water drained from the Fens flows out to sea via the Great Ouse. The name Lynn comes from the Celtic *lindo*, a lake or marshy place. The marshes between the town and The Wash have been drained for arable farming.

Kings Lynn Custom House

The jewel in Lynn's crown is the Custom House. Built in 1683 as a Merchants' Exchange it stands prominently on The Quay. Its style reflects Dutch architecture, trade links with Holland were already strong. In front of the Custom House stands a statue to Captain George Vancouver born in Lynn 1759 and founder of Vancouver, Canada.

References

DYMOND David, *The Norfolk Landscape*, Alastair Press.

HARROD Wilhemine, *The Norfolk Guide*, Alastair Press.

HIGGINS David, *The Beachmen*, Terence Dalton.

JOLLY Cyril, *Henry Blogg of Cromer*, Harrap.

MACMILLAN, *Reeds Nautical Almanac*.

MALSTER Robert, *Saved from the Sea*, Terence Dalton.

MEE Arthur (revised STEPHENSON), *Norfolk*, Hodder & Stoughton.

MEERES Frank, *Not of This World – Norfolk's Monastic Houses*, Meeres.

MORGAN Geoffrey, *East Anglia Tideways and Byways*, Hale.

OPPITZ Leslie, *The Lost Railways of East Anglia*, Countryside Books.

PEVSNER Nikolaus, *The Buildings of England – North East Norfolk & Norwich*, Penguin.

PEVSNER Nikolaus, *The Buildings of North West & South Norfolk*, Penguin.

PIPE Christopher, *The Story of Cromer Pier*, Poppyland Publishing.

ROBINSON Bruce, *Norfolk Fragments*, Elmstead.

ROBINSON Bruce, *The Peddars Way and Norfolk Coast Path*, Countryside.

RYE Walter, *History of Norfolk,* Elliot Stock.

STAGG Frank Noel et al, *Salthouse*, Salthouse History Group.

STIBBONS Peter & CLEVELAND David, *Poppyland*, Poppyland Publishing.

TOOKE Colin, *Great Yarmouth & Gorleston series*, Tookes Books.

WHITE'S, *Norfolk 1845*, David and Charles reprint.